SIMPLY
FAITH
HOPE
& LOVE

by DORIS C. CLARK

Art by ABBY DETRICH

ABOUT THIS PRAYER BOOK

When one of my Joy Class members told me she would like to have a prayer book, I began to search for one with the thought in mind that I would give it to her as a gift. I could not find one that seemed appropriate. The scriptures were too long and complicated with too many thoughts and ideas. The print was too small and many of the words were too difficult to understand. I decided to write my own devotional book for readers on a third grade level with concepts that are more simplified. The result is **SIMPLY FAITH HOPE & LOVE.**

It is my hope that adults with intellectual disabilities, both readers and non-readers, will be able to enjoy this book as well as older adults with cognitive problems and young readers.

It is my prayer that Holy Spirit will open these scriptures to all who study them and fill each life with Christ's love.

Doris Clark

TO DO

**God wants us to read our Bibles each
day and learn how to live the way
God intends us to live.**

**If you are a reader, please take the
time to read one page each day. If
you can't read, ask a friend
to read the page for you.**

**If you read one page each day,
you will have enough scriptures
for a month of reading.**

**May Holy Spirit fill your heart
with Faith, Hope and Love**

1 John 3:1a
Think how much the Father loves us. He loves us so much that he lets us be called his children, as we truly are.

If we are God's children, he is our heavenly Father. As our heavenly Father, God cares for us, loves us, teaches us, and helps us in all things.

Thank you, God, for being our heavenly Father. Amen.

2 Timothy 3:16
[All scripture is "given to us by God" and teaches us, shows us where we are wrong, helps us live better and shows us how to be good.]

It is good to learn as many Bible verses as you can.

Prayer
Thank you, God, for giving us the Bible.
Amen

1 John 3:17
[Whoever has "many things" and sees that another person is in need and refuses to help, does not show that the love of God lives in him or her.]

God's love helps us to share what God has given us with those who don't have enough.

Dear God,
Help us to share what you have given us with others who are in need. In Jesus' name, Amen

Isaiah 40:31
[Those who wait for God to lead
them will have new energy.
They will fly like the eagles.
They will run and not get tired.
They will walk and not be weary.]

It is only by asking God to be with us that
we are able to do things we could not do
alone.

Dear God,
Help us to know how to wait for you to
lead us. Give us your energy to do good for
others and for ourselves. Amen.

1 Thessalonians 5:16-18
Always be joyful and never stop praying. Whatever happens, keep thanking God because of Jesus Christ. This is what God wants you to do.

Talk to God all day long. When you get up say, "Hi, God!" When something good happens, say, "Thank you, God!" When something bad happens, say, "Thank you, God, for being close to me and helping me with this problem!"

Dear God,
Teach me how to rejoice and be glad. And, teach me to pray. Amen

Matthew 7:1-2
[Don't "point out" the wrong things others do and God won't "point out" the wrong things you do. God will be as hard on you as you are on others. He will treat you exactly as you treat them.]

You need to think about your own actions and try to do the right things. Don't worry about what other people are doing.

Lord,
Help me to think about the things you want me to do each day and let you take care of the bad things other people do. Help me to know what others do is none of my business. In Jesus' name, Amen

Psalm 122:1
It made me glad to hear them say, "Let's go to the house of the Lord!"

It is important for us to go to church and worship God. It should make us happy when we go to worship.

Dear God,
Give me joy in worshiping you. Thank you for our church where I can go to worship. Amen.

Mark 7:20-23

Then Jesus said: "What comes from your heart is what makes you unclean. [If your heart is filled with bad thoughts, indecent actions, stealing, murder, unfaithfulness in marriage, meanness, lying, wanting what belongs to someone else, thinking you are better than others, and foolishness, it is not good. All of these can be in your heart and make you unfit to worship God."]

Ask God to make your thoughts and actions right in his sight and to forgive you for your bad thoughts and actions before going to worship.

Dear God, Make my heart clean so that I might worship you. Amen

2 Peter 1:5-8
Do your best to improve your faith [belief in God]. You can do this by adding goodness, understanding, self-control, patience, devotion to God, concern for others and love. If you keep growing in this way, it will show that what you know about our Lord, Jesus Christ has made your lives useful and meaningful.

These things are called virtues or good things to help us live better lives. Look at each one and see how you can add them to your life.

Dear God, Help me to grow in good things so that others may know that Jesus is making my life wonderful. In Jesus' name, Amen

Isaiah 41:10

Don't be afraid! I am with you. Don't tremble with fear! I am your God. I will make you strong, as I protect you with my arm and give you victories.

God is always with you. What a wonderful promise. You don't have to be afraid. Trust in God. Trust in the strength he gives you.

Dear Heavenly Father,
Take away my fear and help me to know that you are with me now. Help me to trust you more each day. Thank you for loving me. In Jesus' name, Amen

Romans 8:38-39
I am sure that nothing can separate us from God's love—not life or death, not angels or spirits, not the present or the future, and not powers above or powers below. Nothing in all creation can separate us from God's love for us in Christ Jesus our Lord!

God will always be with you because you believe in Jesus. This is a promise. You should not be afraid but be thankful for God's amazing promise of love.

Dear God,
Thank you for telling me that nothing can separate me from your love. Help me to live my life trusting you and showing your love to others. In the name of Jesus, Amen

Isaiah 44:2a
[God said:] "I am your Creator. You were in my care even before you were born."

God made the world and everything in it. That includes you. He knows you — everything about you. You are important to him. He will take care of you.

Dear God,
Thank you for making me. Thank you for loving me. Thank you for taking care of me. Help me to remember that you love me. In Jesus' name, Amen

Matthew 6:14-15

[Jesus said:] "If you forgive others for the wrongs they do to you, your Father in heaven will forgive you. But if you don't forgive others, your Father will not forgive your sins.

If someone does something wrong to you like telling lies about you, being rude to you, stealing from you, or making fun of you, God expects you to forgive that person. That is hard to do but it is very important to do that. If you want God to forgive your mistakes you must forgive the mistakes of others.

Dear God,
I know I can forgive others only if you help me. Give me your love in my heart for everyone, even those who do wrong things. Thank you, Dear Father, Amen.

Romans 12:9-10

Be sincere in your love for others. Hate everything that is evil and hold tight to everything that is good. Love each other as brothers and sisters and honor others more than you do yourself.

I need to think about doing good things all the time and stop even thinking about doing wrong things. Help me to love the people I am with each day like they are my brothers and sisters and really mean it.

Dear God,
Help me to love other people. Help me to think about doing good things and not wrong things. Thank you for sending Jesus to show me how to love.
In the name of Jesus, Amen

John 14:21
[Jesus said:] "If you love me, you will do what I have said, and my Father will love you. I will also love you and show you what I am like."

I need to read my Bible and go to church so that I can know what Jesus has said. Then I can do what Jesus tells me to do.

Dear God,
Help me to love Jesus and to do what he wants me to do. Help me to go to church and read my Bible so that I can understand what to do. Thank you for for loving me. In the name of Jesus, Amen

Psalm 139:1-2
You have looked deep into my heart, Lord, and you know all about me. You know when I am resting or when I am working, and from heaven you discover my thoughts.

I need to remember that God knows what I am doing all the time. I need to try to have good thoughts and to do good things so God will smile when he sees me.

Dear God,
Help me to have your love in my heart so I can make you smile today. Thank you for caring about me. In the name of Jesus, Amen

Psalm 23:1
You, Lord, are my shepherd, I will never be in need.

God will take care of my needs. I don't have to worry about anything. If I will trust God and love Jesus, I will have everything I need.

Dear God,
Help me to trust you in all things. Thank you for the promises you give me in your Bible. Help me to not worry or be afraid. In Jesus' name, Amen

1 John 4:9-10
God showed his love for us when he sent his only son into the world to give us life. Real love isn't our love for God, but his love for us. God sent his son to [give his life so our sins could be forgiven.]

How wonderful to know that God loves me so much. I need to tell others about God's love for them and about Jesus who died and rose again to give us new life.

Dear God,
Thank you and praise to you for the love you give to me. Help me to love you back and to tell others about your great love.
In Jesus' name, Amen

1 Peter 5:7
God cares for you, so turn all your worries over to him.

To sit and worry about your problems means you are not trusting God to help you. Show your faith in God by telling him about your worries and letting him take care of you.

Dear God,
Help me to trust you enough to let you take care of me. Thank you for loving me and caring what happens to me.
In the name of Jesus, Amen

Matthew 28:20
[Jesus said:]
I will be with you always, even until the end of the world.

This is a great promise to you. It means you will never be alone. Jesus will always be with you. You don't have to be afraid or lonely. Jesus will be with you to help you know what to do and how to do it. You have a wonderful friend and brother.

Dear God,
Thank you for Jesus. Thank you for promising that you will always be with me. Help me to do what you want me to do. Thank you for making me your child. Amen

Matthew 11:28-30

[Jesus said:] "If you are tired from carrying heavy burdens, come to me and I will give you rest. Take the yoke I give you. Put it on your shoulders and learn from me. I am gentle and humble, and you will find rest. This yoke is easy to bear, and this burden is light."

Yokes were used around an animal's shoulder to make the animal go where its owner wanted it to go. Jesus is saying that he will give you guidance and expect service from you that is easy because he is with you to help you.

Dear God,
Help me to serve you in all that I do.
Teach me to let you help me with all my troubles and concerns.
In Jesus' name, Amen

Luke 1:46-48
Mary said: With all my heart I praise the Lord, and I am glad because of God, my Savior. He cares for me his humble servant. From now on all people will say God has blessed me.

I need to praise God each day as Mary did after she was told she would be the mother of Jesus.

Dear God,
Give me the words to praise your name and give you thanks for everything you have done for me. In the name of Jesus, Amen

Isaiah 41:13
I am the Lord your God. I am holding your hand so don't be afraid. I am here to help you.

When life gets hard and you feel scared and alone, remember that God is with you holding your hand. Trust him to help you.

Dear God,
Sometimes it is hard to remember that you are holding my hand. When I get scared and sad, help me to know that you are there to help me. Thank you for loving me. In Jesus' name, Amen

John 3:16
God loved the people of this world so much that he gave his only Son, so that everyone who has faith in him will have eternal life and never really die.

Because God loves us, Jesus died for us and rose again so that we could live forever.

Dear God,
Thank you for your love for me. Help me to live my life the way you want me to live it. Thank you for Jesus. Amen.

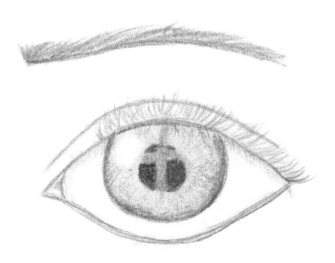

1 John 3:9 & 10

God's children cannot keep on being sinful. His life-giving power lives in them and makes them his children, so that they cannot keep on sinning. You can tell God's children from the devil's children, because those who belong to the devil refuse to do right or to love each other.

When you have choices to make about good things or bad things, you will want to do good things if you are a child of God.

Lord, help me to make good choices this day. Help me to be filled with your love and know that I am your child. In the name of Jesus, Amen

Philippians 4:8
Finally, brothers and sisters, whatever is true, whatever is honorable, whatever is right, whatever is pure, whatever is lovely, whatever is good, think about those things.

If you always think of things that are good, your life will look like good things. If you always think of things that are bad or ugly, your life will look bad.

Dear God,
Help me to think of the good things around me. Amen

Ephesians 4: 31-32
[Let all bad feelings and anger and hate and lie-telling be put away from you. And be kind to one another, forgiving each other just as God through Jesus has forgiven you.]

Be filled with kindness and don't be mean to others. Don't tell lies about anyone. Forgive others when they have done something bad to you.

Dear God,
Help me to be a kind person. Teach me how to forgive others who have been unkind to me. Amen

James 5:13
[Is anyone among you suffering? (sad or sick)
Let him or her pray. Is anyone cheerful?
(happy) Let him or her sing praises.]

God has promised to help us when we are
sad. I need to remember that.

Lord,
Teach me to pray and help me to be cheerful
and sing your praises. Amen

James 4:17
[If you know the right thing to do and don't do it, you have sinned.]

Read the Bible, listen to teachers and pastors in order to learn the right things to do.

Dear God,
Help me to learn your way and forgive me when I don't follow your teachings. Amen.

1 John 4:21
The commandment that God has given us is: Love God and love each other.

It is hard to love people who are mean to us, but God can help us.

Thank you God for showing us your love in Jesus. Amen.

**REMEMBER, GOD LOVES YOU
JUST THE WAY YOU ARE!**

THIS BOOK IS GIVEN TO YOU IN THE HOPE THAT YOU MAY GROW IN GOD'S LOVE AND UNDERSTANDING

NOTES

NOTES

CPSIA information can be obtained at www.ICGtesting.com
Printed in the USA
LVOW01s0803120913

352115LV00010B/26/P